Explorer mazes

Explorer mazes

maze craze

Sterling Publishing Co., Inc.
New York

Library of Congress Cataloging-in-Publication Data Available

10   9   8   11/2009

Published in 2004 by Sterling Publishing Co., Inc.
387 Park Avenue South, New York, NY 10016
Originally published in Germany in 2004 under the title
Expedition ins Dschungelreich by Edition Bücherbär im Arena
Verlag GmbH, Rottendorfer Str. 16, D-97074 Würzburg
Copyright © 2004 by Edition Bücherbär im Arena Verlag GmbH
English translation by Daniel M. Shea and Nicole Franke
English translation © 2004 by Sterling Publishing Co., Inc.
Distributed in Canada by Sterling Publishing
c/o Canadian Manda Group, 165 Dufferin Street
Toronto, Ontario, Canada M6K 3H6
Distributed in Great Britain and Europe by Chris Lloyd at Orca Book
Services, Stanley House, Fleets Lane, Poole BH15 3AJ, England
Distributed in Australia by Capricorn Link (Australia) Pty Ltd.
P.O. Box 704, Windsor, NSW 2756, Australia

Sterling ISBN-13: 978-1-4027-1757-4
        ISBN-10: 1-4027-1757-1
For information about custom editions, special sales, premium and
corporate purchases, please contact Sterling Special Sales
Department at 800-805-5489 or specialsales@sterlingpub.com

Draw a picture or place a
photograph of yourself here.

This book belongs to:

_____

This is Mr. Smith and his dog Oliver.
Mr. Smith is a butterfly collector.

Mr. Smith lives in a big house. He is very rich and would be perfectly happy if only he wasn't missing the most beautiful butterfly from his collection: the blue and purple King Shoemaker butterfly. Can you find your way through his collection?

end

start

Mr. Smith is flying to Africa today in a steel-blue airplane. The African jungle is the only place where he can find the rare King Shoemaker butterfly. Help him get there.

start

end

Follow Mr. Smith on a steamer up the river to start his search.

A strange flag flutters above the small trade station in the middle of the jungle. Move from start to finish by counting from one to nine in order. When you get to nine, start at the next number one. Don't skip numbers!

start

end

Some baby turtles just hatched on the beach and Mr. Smith is trying to figure out which turtle crawled out of each sand hole. Can you help him?

Mr. Smith's path is blocked by creepers. Can you help him get through this dense tangle of plants? Make sure you don't move against the direction in which the arrows point.

end

start

A swampy stretch of water lies in front of Mr. Smith and Oliver. In order to cross it, they will have to balance on top of the overturned tree trunks. Can you help them find their way?

start

end

A crocodile is lying in wait for Mr. Smith and Oliver. Fortunately, Mr. Smith has a can of sausages with him, which immediately tames the crocodile. Oliver gets a sausage as well.

start

end

A gigantic tree stands in a clearing. Can you find the way from the trunk to the birds' nest?

In the afternoon, Mr. Smith and Oliver find a giant tangle of snakes. Can you make heads or tails of this?

end

start

Mr. Smith and Oliver need to reach the other side of a large lake. Luckily, a nice hippopotamus gives them a ride on his back and they are able to get across quickly.

start

end

Mischievous monkeys are waiting for Mr. Smith and Oliver on the other side of the lake. Which monkey climbs on each rope?

When Mr. Smith gets out of the jungle, he finds a giant elephant blocking the path. Fortunately, the elephant only glances at him and then continues to peacefully chew its food.

After a long hike along the river, the adventurers find themselves at the top of a large waterfall. Moving only in the direction the arrows are pointing, find your way out of this tricky situation.

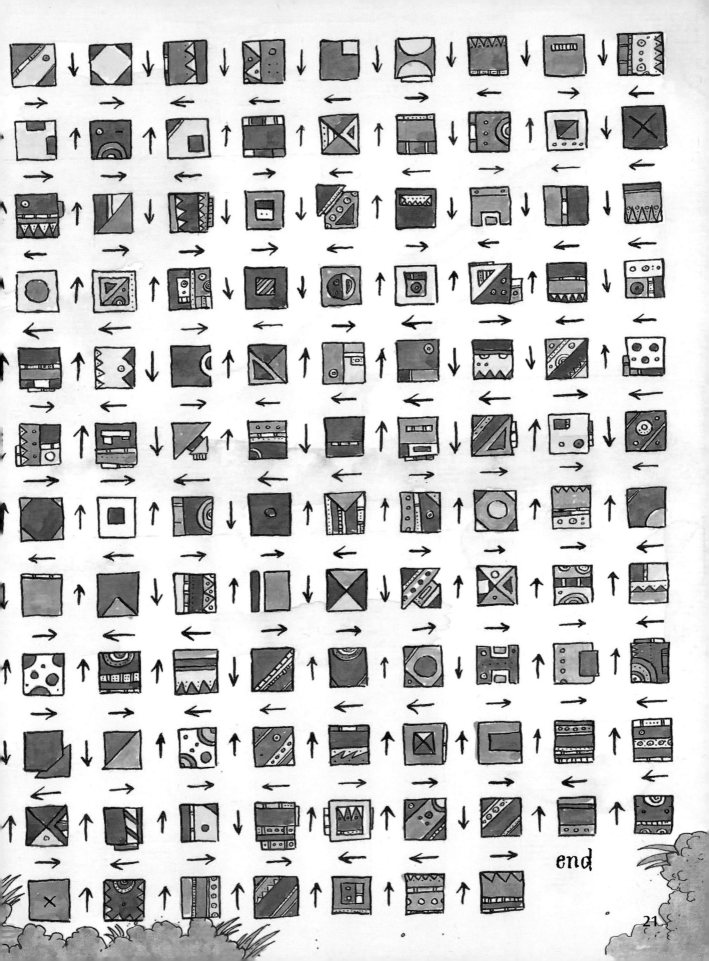

end

21

When Mr. Smith emerges from the trees, he frightens a flock of colorful parrots.
Can you figure out where each parrot started?

Mr. Smith and Oliver are hungry. A friendly gorilla shows them the best way to some bananas. Use the arrows to guide you through the maze. Make sure you don't move against the direction in which the arrows point.

start

end

Guide only the animal that lives in the jungle to the finish. Do you know where the other animals live?

start?

penguin

start?

kangaroo

end

start?

elephant

start?

elk

Mr. Smith discovers a remote jungle village. Perhaps the inhabitants will know something about the King Shoemaker butterfly. Mr. Smith decides to search if anyone is there. Start at the red hut and see how fast you can get to the blue hut.

No one is home. Mr. Smith finds a collection of African dance masks and takes a minute to admire them before moving on. Follow the masks with the bones to see which is his favorite.

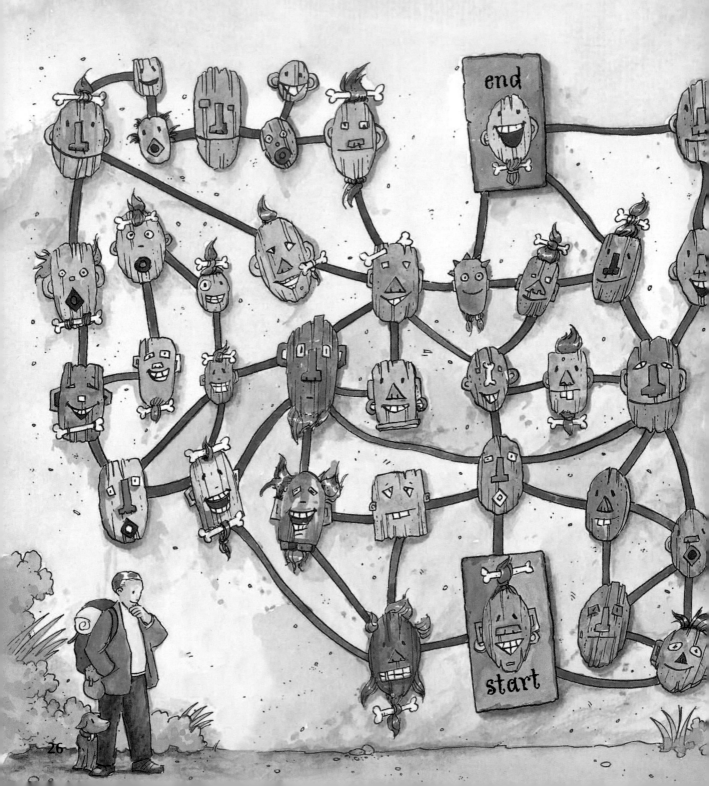

Mr. Smith comes to a rocky gorge where he discovers a butterfly. Is it the right one?

The old hanging bridge looks shaky, but Mr. Smith does not give up!

start

end

Mr. Smith finally discovers the King Shoemaker butterfly in a kaleidoscope of butterflies. Help him catch it with his net.

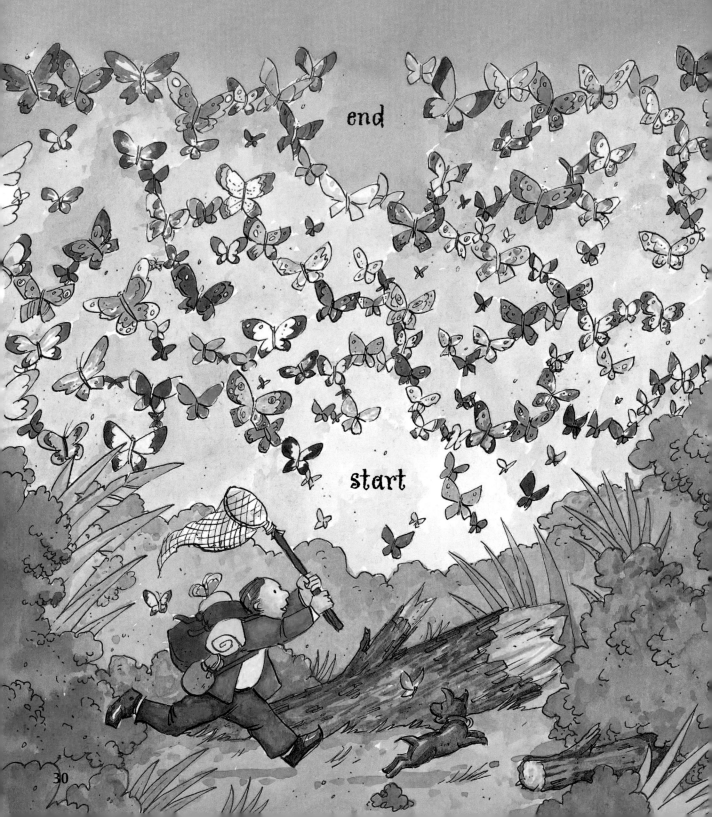

Mr. Smith observes the butterfly for a long time but finally realizes that the jungle is its home and sets it free again. How does Mr. Smith find his own way back?

start

end

Mr. Smith didn't keep the butterfly, but his trip was not for nothing. He had many exciting adventures and made some new friends.

Back at home, Mr. Smith decides to start a new collection: African dance masks.

end

start

Answers

page 6

page 7

page 8

page 9

34

1 = D
2 = A
3 = B
4 = E
5 = C

pages 12–13

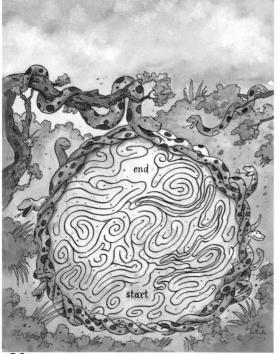

A = 4
B = 3
C = 1
D = 2

pages 20–21

A = 3
B = 1
C = 5
D = 4
E = 2

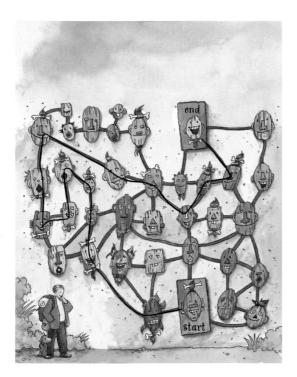

pages 28–29